GW00363920

The reflections of the office towers of the city of Perth, seen from Mount Bay Road, shimmer in the ripples of the Swan River.

Business and recreation are never far apart in Perth.

Burswood Casino is an adornment to the Perth scene.

To see the sights along the Swan as you travel, take a leisurely ferry ride.

PERTH

Perth is a beautiful city with a charm all its own. Basking on the banks of the broad and sinuous Swan River, in the relatively warm winters and hot summers of a Mediterranean climate, this capital of the west is a warm and friendly city, with a wealth of attractions.

Perth residents take full advantage of the high quality of life the city affords and of the opportunities to enjoy an outdoor lifestyle. Along with the physical, Perth has a thriving intellectual and cultural life nurtured by well planned and accessible facilities such as the Art Gallery, Concert Hall, and Museum.

In the business heart of the city, gleaming office towers and the architectural remnants of a colonial past give an air of prosperity and confidence to one of the world's most isolated capitals. Perth's crowning glory, Kings Park, offers landscaped gardens blending with natural bushland within a stone's throw of the city centre. At the mouth of the Swan, the historic sea port of Fremantle is now almost part of Perth, linked by fast-growing suburbs.

Above: *The spectacle of Australia Day fireworks over the city.*
Over: *From Kings Park, the city skyline glows at dusk.*

PERTH

From the air, Perth's geography becomes apparent. The Swan River divides the city and the central business district sits on the broad expanse of Perth Water which opens out from The Narrows. Tall buildings jostle for attention as reminders of the state's mineral wealth and Perth's role as administrative capital of Australia's largest state. Perth's suburbs spread in all directions, bounded in the west by the Indian Ocean.

To the north of the city centre, in Northbridge, beats the heart of Perth's nightlife. The Perth Cultural Centre complex, the Art Gallery of Western Australia, the Alexander Library and the Western Australian Museum are also in Northbridge. These and other centres are the venues for the Festival of Perth, an annual feast of visual arts, literature, drama, dance, music and film.

Over the Narrows Bridge and off the Kwinana Freeway is the Perth Zoo, set in beautiful gardens that can also be reached by crossing Perth Water by ferry.

Above: *Kwinana Freeway through South Perth to southern suburbs.*

The Narrows, western gateway to Perth city and suburbs.

A well planned system of roadways makes the city easily accessible.

An efficient public transport network links the city and suburbs.

Subiaco Oval, host to, among other sports, Australian Rules football.

Hay Street Mall, the city's retail heart, offers a range of shopping and dining experiences.

ondon Court, a taste of Olde England in the city.

Through the Tudor archway in Hay Street Mall is London Court.

Murray Street Mall offers a haven from busy city traffic.

An African performer entertains the crowds in Murray Street Mall.

PERTH SHOPPING

Serious shoppers, locals and visitors, are well catered for in Perth's retail heart. From major department stores to exclusive speciality shops, the city has the lot. Popular Hay Street, Murray Street and Forrest Place malls, linked by arcades and side streets, attract throngs of shoppers who are likely to be entertained by performers and musicians from many lands. London Court, with its distinctive half-timbered Tudor-style architecture, was built in 1937 for Claude Albo de Bernales. It houses a variety of shops, and the jousting knights which ornament the clocks above its entrances never fail to fascinate passers-by.

Over: The paddlewheeler 'Decoy' against the city skyline at dawn.

PERTH: PAST AND PRESENT

Captain James Stirling's enthusiastic reports to his superiors in England in 1826 led to a migration rush of free settlers to the Swan River district. Following the founding of the colony in 1829, however, times were lean for the new settlers. The acceptance of convicts for ten years from 1850 provided the labour force to construct roads, bridges and public buildings, but it was not until gold and other minerals were discovered later in the century that Perth really prospered.

Today, Perth is a thriving state capital and the city has benefited from a building expansion which was fuelled by the resources boom of the 1970s and 1980s. Although much of the city was rebuilt, there remain some delightful old buildings which serve as a reminder of days gone by.

Above: *Perth, a well planned and prosperous city, from the air.*
Left: *Many old buildings have been restored. This one is in King Street.*
Opposite: *A restored heritage building amid the modern city high-rise.*

Bank West, St Georges Terrace, is fronted by the former Palace Hotel with its gracious facade and iron lace balconies.

His Majesty's Theatre, Hay Street.

Old Perth Boys School.

Perth GPO, Forrest Mall.

The former Perth Court of Petty Sessions.

REMINDERS OF TIMES PAST

Many of the city's fine old buildings retain their grace and elegance although often they have new functions. The Gothic-style Old Perth Boys' School, built in 1854, is now a gift shop. The opulent His Majesty's Theatre, opened in 1904, is a fine example of theatre architecture. These beautiful examples of the design and building skills of times past continue to serve late twentieth century needs and give a sense of Perth's history.

Stained-glass window, Forrest Chase Shopping Centre.

The heights of Central Park, Perth's tallest building.

The past is mirrored in the present, Central Park.

Reflections in Central Park.

REFLECTIONS

The grand buildings of times past are joined now by modern architectural forms, buildings which reflect today's desires and needs. Yet even the newest buildings look to the past for ideas: stained-glass windows are still popular today, modern designs ensuring that the art form stays alive. Many buildings reflect the culture of Perth in a more literal sense also, with sheets of mirrored glass enabling the city to see itself echoed in the shining panes.

Wesley Uniting Church, with Central Park in the rear.

FUN ON THE SWAN

Living in a city which has weather perfect for outdoor activities, Perth people like nothing more than to unwind on a fine weekend with a relaxing picnic on the banks of the Swan or in one of the many parks and gardens for which Perth is renowned. Many favourite spots have the city as a backdrop across Perth Water, the broad reach of the Swan River on which Perth stands, including the riverbank parks of South Perth and the ever-popular Kings Park.

Top: *Many parks and gardens have picnic facilities which are popular with family groups on weekends.*
Above: *A stroll along the banks of the Swan, in South Perth, provides a great view of the city skyline.*
Left: *People relax and enjoy the superb weather while waiting for the evening fireworks display on Australia Day.*

The flotilla of sailing vessels competing in weekend events in perfect weather on the Swan.

A catamaran skims over the Swan.

Children enjoy the quiet waters of Matilda Bay.

Jetskiers enjoying themselves on the Swan.

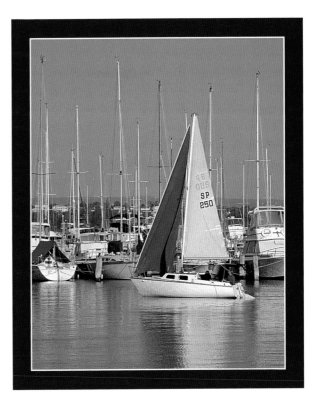

BOATING

Sailing vessels have been coming to the Western Australian coast for hundreds of years. In the sixteenth century, Dutch ships travelled up the coast, sometimes foundering, on their journeys to Batavia. With the establishment of a British colony in the nineteenth century, sailing ships were the only means of communication and supply for the new settlers.

Today, the protected waters of the Swan River provide ideal boating conditions. The number of craft out at any time attests to the popularity of boating of all persuasions, from the relaxation of a leisurely trip under sail or motor, to an exciting race, to the thrill of the speed of jetskis.

In 1983, *Australia II*, a yacht owned by Perth businessman Alan Bond, raced in the United States to become the first 12-metre yacht to wrest the America's Cup from the Americans in 132 years. When the Cup was defended in Fremantle in 1987, the eyes of the world were on Perth.

Above: *Matilda Bay Marina.*
Over: *Catamarans on the Swan against the city skyline.*
Pages 24-25: *Coffee Point Marina, Melville Water.*

The state flag proudly features the Union Jack and a black swan.

The state crest adorns government offices.

Seagulls jostle hopefully when the swans are fed on the banks of the Swan River.

THE BLACK SWANS

The Swan River was named in 1696 by the Dutch Captain Willem de Vlamingh after the black swans he found there. These graceful birds are common to other states, but they particularly signify Western Australia. They are the faunal emblem of the state and they appear on flags and crests around the city. Black swans, which breed in all months of the year, are often seen in family groups and both sexes share the task of incubating the eggs and rearing the young. A group of downy cygnets, which take many months to attain the dark colour, are often seen swimming after their parents.

Opposite: The black swans of the fountain appear to take flight while the real birds and their cygnets swim peacefully in the Citizen of the Year Lake at Burswood Casino.

KINGS PARK

Perth's superb city park is an oasis of nature and a botanical treasure trove. In its natural bushland, animals such as euros and possums live in proximity to the bustling city. Sitting on the grassy slopes of Kings Park, surrounded by wildflowers and listening to birdsong, is a good way to forget the cares of the world. Far beyond the city skyline, the Darling Ranges rise out of the fertile plains of the interior.

Nearer, the towering office buildings and busy streets contrast with the serenity of the tranquil Swan River which is more often than not dotted with sailing craft. Many people cycle, drive, walk or jog in this park, while others explore or just sit and meditate in this sanctuary within the city.

Above: *Fraser's Restaurant, Kings Park.*
Opposite: *Kings Park at dusk, looking towards the city.*

28

KINGS PARK

Wandering the paths of Kings Park on foot is one way to enjoy its visual pleasure, or visitors can ride in a horse-drawn carriage. At every turn there is something to discover – a new vista, magnificent botanical specimens in the open air or in glasshouses and arboretums.

A horse and carriage ride (right) is a fine way to see the park.
Kings Park lookouts (left and below right) provide ideal vantage points from which to admire the city skyline.
Below are the War Memorial and the Wishing Well.

Nature trail, Kings Park.

Panoramic view from Kings Park.

KINGS PARK

Nature trails allow visitors to enjoy the sights, sounds and scents of the bush. Honeyeaters, parrots and a host of other birds frequent the park and can be seen flocking when abundant nectar is available on the stands of native species which are a feature of the park. When the wildflowers are blooming, Kings Park is ablaze with colour.

Left: *A drive down Fraser Avenue, lined with lemon-scented gums, can lead to idyllic picnic spots.*
Opposite: *The views within Kings Park and without are equally beautiful.*

WILDFLOWERS

Western Australia is justly famed for its wildflowers. Visitors make special pilgrimages to the best places, from August to November, when the seasonal flowers carpet the countryside with colour. They grow in profusion in Perth's many parks, including Kings Park, and in the reserves and national parks not far from the city. From the woodlands to the open plains and the coastal heathlands, wildflowers, from delicate orchids to hardy banksias, present a brilliant display. There are over 3000 species in the south-west of the state and many of these are widespread. Others occur only in specific regions, or even in single locations.

Top: *Wehlia.*
Above: *Many-flowered fringed lily.*
Right: *Wildflowers blanket the ground with colour.*

Scarlet banksia.

Cowslip orchid.

Spring blossoms are scattered like jewels among the greenery of Kings Park's carefully tended gardens.

Kings Park comes alive in springtime, with blooms lining walkways and lawns.

King spider orchid.

Mangles' kangaroo paw.

AT THE BEACH

Perth is bounded on the west by the Indian Ocean, and Perth residents take full advantage of the long, broad sweeps of sandy beaches, the rolling breakers of the ocean and the sheltered waters in the lee of Rottnest and other islands. There are several popular ocean beaches, including Cottesloe, City and Scarborough Beaches. The suburbs stretch to the seafront, and access to beaches, the popular ones and those that are less crowded, is easy. The Perth weather, too, is a great inducement to surf and sunbathe.

Top: *Brightly coloured umbrellas dot the sand as beach-goers relax by the sea.*
Above and left: *Scarborough Beach aerials from the city and from the ocean. The landmark Observation City Complex houses apartments, restaurants and shops.*

Bathing in front of the Pavilion, Cottesloe Beach.

A red and yellow flag of the Surf Life Saving Association signals a safe swimming area at Cottesloe Beach.

The sheltered beach at Cottesloe is protected by a rock wall.

City Beach from the air, with the Darling Ranges in the background.

Hillarys Boat Harbour, Sorrento, offers sheltered moorings.

Relaxing on Hillarys Beach opposite Sorrento Quay.

Lifesavers, in their familiar red and yellow garb.

Adjoining Marmion Marine Park, Hillarys Boat Harbour at Sorrento, north of Fremantle, offers sheltered moorings, a white-sand beach, and Sorrento Quay lined with restaurants and shops. In the oceanarium, Underwater World, visitors are surrounded by the creatures of the ocean as they walk through a submerged tunnel.

Over: *At the historic port of Fremantle at the mouth of the Swan are Success, Fishing Boat, Challenger and Inner Harbours, providing berths for watercraft of all shapes and sizes, from pleasure craft to container ships.*

White sands and cool ocean waters at City Beach.

The replica of a tram travels past the facades of historic buildings.

The ornate grandeur of the City Hall.

Queens Buildings, another example of the past adapting to the present.

The broad verandas of the fully restored Esplanade Hotel.

The Round House, WA's first prison, quarried from local stone.

The National Hotel.

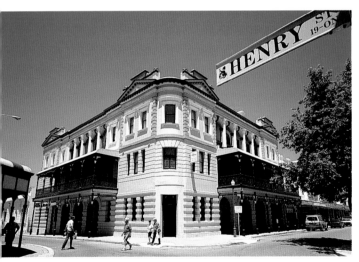

The Orient Hotel.

Fremantle Railway Station.

FREMANTLE

In 1829, Captain Charles Howe Fremantle claimed "the whole of the west coast of New Holland in the name of King George". After 20 years of colonisation, the free settlers at this port at the mouth of the Swan were struggling economically. Convicts were accepted from Britain and their labour constructed many of the city's historic buildings, some of which still stand. As the site of the America's Cup Challenge in 1987, Fremantle gained a reputation as an international tourist destination. It remains a maritime city, though it provides more berths for pleasure craft than for commercial shipping. Today, "Freo" is a cosmopolitan city with a unique charm, home to a warm, friendly, multicultural community.

Cafes on Fremantle's "cappuccino strip" at dusk.

Geordie Bay settlement.

Thomson Bay settlement viewed over the Bathurst Light.

The cool clear water of Rottnest Island.

A perfect beach on Rottnest Island, a popular holiday destination.

Rottnest Island, a carefully managed public reserve.

Boating is a popular island activity.

ROTTNEST ISLAND

Rottnest Island was originally named by the Dutch Captain Willem de Vlamingh for the animals he took to be large rats, actually quokkas. A prison for mainland Aborigines was established here by British colonists in 1838. Located 20 km west of Fremantle and reached by sea or by air, the island accommodates more than a million visitors a year. This sandy island has been declared a public reserve, and wise management has ensured that bicycles rule here with vehicular traffic having been restricted. Some of the southernmost coral reefs in the world are found off Rottnest, and there are a number of shipwrecks. The charm of the island is in the peace of its gleaming white beaches, bays, secluded coves and sparkling turquoise waters.

Right: *One of Rottnest's famous quokkas.*

Monkey Mia is renowned for its friendly bottlenose dolphins.

Monkey Mia, Peron Peninsula.

Francois Peron National Park, Shark Bay.

MONKEY MIA

About 800 km north of Perth, in the shallow waters of Shark Bay on the central coast of Western Australia, an adventurous small group of bottlenose dolphins come close to shore to the delight of the thousands of visitors who come to Monkey Mia for this unique form of human-animal interaction. These inquisitive wild animals swim up to the beach, regularly in winter, less so in summer, where eager humans can observe them at close quarters and, if they're lucky, feed them.

Living further out in the clear green-blue waters of Shark Bay World Heritage and Marine Park are about 300 dolphins who catch fish, court, breed and raise their young in the sheltered area which includes the vast Wooramel seagrass bank. Here also are a large number of marine animals, including the rare dugong, a shy animal which, unlike the dolphins, shuns attention. At nearby Hamelin Pool are stromatolites, one of the oldest forms of microbial life in the world.

The importance of the physical environment and its wildlife were recognised worldwide with its listing as a World Heritage area.

Bottlenose dolphins being admired and fed at Monkey Mia.

The Murchison River, Kalbarri National Park.

The rugged landscape of Mt Augustus.

Whalebone Bay, Fitzgerald River National Park.

The Pilbara region, covered with spring blooms.

The Pinnacles, Nambung National Park, are masses of weathered limestone pillars set in a desert of golden sand.

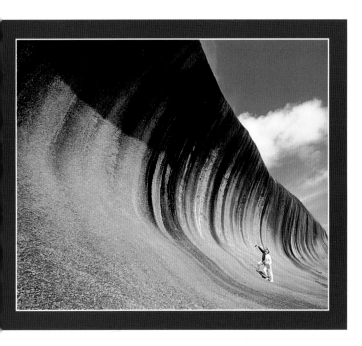

WESTERN AUSTRALIA

Western Australia, the largest of Australia's States, is big in area, big in natural riches and big in personality. In its wild places Nature's drama and diversity are on display – in vast deserts, in ancient landforms wonderfully wrought by the elements, in the massed colours of wildflowers that carpet the landscape in springtime. Many spectacular natural features are conserved in national and marine parks which also harbour unique animal and plant life. In its cities, towns and resorts lifestyles run the gamut, from international sophistication to the simple life. And all this comes with a welcoming warmth and friendliness that is particularly Western Australian.

Left: Wave Rock, a unique rock formation near Hyden in the south-west.

Perth, reflected in Perth Water at dawn.